MY PURGE STORY

A FIRST HAND ACCOUNT FROM A GAY PURGE SURVIVOR

LCol (Ret'd) Steven P. Deschamps, CD

DEDICATION

This book is dedicated to Captain (Ret'd) Pat Mulhall, former CO of 103 Thunderbird Squadron, Royal Canadian Air Cadets North Vancouver, who, when I decided to re-enrol in the Canadian Forces to challenge the law, was my Commanding Officer. She knows why!

To all survivors and victims who experienced the Purge. We are comrades, lost to each other because of the Official Secrets Act, never knowing of each other's fate until 2017 when the Prime Minister apologized to us in the House of Commons. More than 7500 were expected to join the class action suit, with less than 730 actually engaging. I dedicate my story to you. You will understand even though you don't know me. And I know you, even though I don't know your story. In service together now, we can hold our heads high!

Kerry and Pat Mulhall (left) at my Canada Pride Citation presentation April 2023 along with VAdm Topshee, LCol Kevin Leblond and CWO Justin Harper, 443 Sqn. (CFB Esquimalt Imaging Unit)

Library and Archives Canada Cataloguing in Publication
Deschamps, Steven P, author
My Purge Story / Steven P. Deschamps

Funding in part for this book was provided by a grant from the LGTB Purge Fund. Le financement de ce livre a été en partie assuré par une subvention du LGTB Purge Fund

Issued in print and electronic formats.
ISBN: 978-1-998501-02-1 (paperback)
ISBN: 978-1-998501-03-8 (ebook)

Editor: James Leslie
Cover Design: Leif Halton
Interior Design: Muhammad Tahir

Warpath Press
Toronto, Ontario, Canada
www.warpathpress.com

TABLE OF CONTENTS

FOREWORD

When I was thirteen years old, I loved to sneak into the cellar of the family home in Cornwall, Ontario and dress up in my older brothers' Air Cadet uniforms. I loved how it felt, and I knew that I was destined for a career in the Air Force. Who could have known that this love would turn into betrayal, polygraphs, and years of denial and depression for a little boy who still had no idea he was gay in 1969.

Chapter 1

MY TEENS

My father died of sepsis from a diverticulitis operation that went south when I was thirteen. It was 1969. I remember watching him slowly wilt away from his bedside in the Cornwall General hospital as the unknown surgical nick in his bowel slowly took his life away. He suffered with pain continuously until it was decided he would be moved to Kingston, where he could get better care at the university hospital. He died of a blood clot within weeks. My father had been the centre of our family. A firm but fair man, whose charm and wit made him the social convener of our neighbourhood. He was a Combat Engineer Warrant Officer Second Class, and Sergeant Major of the Combat Engineer school in Petawawa during the war.

My first exposure to a dead person was my father. At thirteen years of age, I attended the Cornwall Funeral Home and walked into the big room with my father lying in an open casket, surrounded by walls of flowers. At thirteen you don't understand death, nor can you understand how it can happen to your father. I had seen him a week or so before his death in Kingston Hospital. He was emaciated and thin and had been transferred to the palliative care unit after suffering a brain stem vascular incident. My mother told me he would be coming home soon

1

Mom and Dad's wedding in Petawawa, 1943. (Author's Photo)

and I remember thinking "How would they let someone out of the hospital in his condition?" When I saw him again at the funeral home, a family friend and owner of the funeral home, Ray Sullivan, had restored my father's body, making it look like he was in perfect health, something the doctors could not do. My father looked great; unfortunately, he was dead.

Perhaps I was inspired by his strength or his wit. It's not unusual for a son to want to follow in his father's footsteps and I always wanted to grow up to be like my dad. I joined Cornwall's 325 Squadron of the Royal Canadian Air Cadets in the fall of 1969.

The toll of my father's death left me troubled but I found new energy in my involvement in the Air Cadets. I was an outgoing teenager, school president in grade eight, popular among my peers, but I struggled with having a deep, dark, secret. I didn't know what that was, but I was acutely aware of the bullies and the loudmouths that used fag jokes to make them feel popular or important. I didn't date girls and, in my early teens, always found myself around guys where I was most comfortable. That's not out of the ordinary for young teenagers. My sexuality was arrested, or I was just too afraid to experiment. For me, that would be crossing that taboo line into being gay. And In the early 1970s, the last thing a teenager wanted to be was labelled a faggot.

In 1969, homosexuality was decriminalized as a criminal offence in Canada. It wasn't until 1982 that the Charter of Rights and Freedoms was signed and, in 1986, sexual orientation was enshrined, making employment discrimination illegal for gays and lesbians. It wasn't until 1992 that the Canadian Armed Forces started accepting openly gay men and women in the military, and that was only because they were forced to by the Federal Court of Canada under the terms of the Michelle Douglas settlement.

The reality in the 70s was that it was simply not safe to be gay, let alone think you could be accepted. Newspapers often reported beatings and assaults on gay people. Employers would shun you if you were effeminate or flamboyant and prejudice was everywhere. If you came out, you could expect contempt, harassment, physical and mental assaults, and death threats.

That's where the Air Cadets came to save my teens. In Air Cadets, everyone dressed in the Air Cadet uniform. Style and wealth were left at the clothing supply door and you were issued uniforms that made everyone look the same. Girls had not been introduced to the cadets, that wouldn't come for another five or six years, and outside of the very few Neanderthals that made it into cadets, we felt a wonderful sense of belonging. Rank and the shine on your boots played the most important role in your sense of belonging and esteem, and I fit in rather well. The Air Cadet squadron I belonged to was well run, led by older teenage cadets who were positive role models, and the officer volunteers became my heroes. I went to my first summer camp in 1971 at the age of fifteen at CFB Bagotville, in the Saguenay area of Quebec. I loved it. Being on an Air Force base made me feel like I had found my home. The roar of CF 101 Voodoo fighter jets, the mess halls, the rigour of cadet life, all were totally natural for me. Being a pilot was shaping up as my ultimate goal and becoming an Air Force officer was my destiny. I remember setting my objectives that summer at Bagotville; I would become the best at whatever I did. For cadets, that meant I set my goals on becoming the Warrant Officer 1st Class, the top ranking cadet.

When I returned to Cornwall at the end of the summer of 1971, I marched into the Cornwall Armouries like I owned the place. It must have been obvious to the others too as I was promoted from Leading Air Cadet to Flight Sergeant, three promotions in seven months. By the time summer camp selection was made at the end of training for the 1971-72 year, I was awarded two trophies for proficiency and selected to go to the coveted Senior Leaders Course (SLC) at the Canadian Forces Base in Borden, Ontario that summer.

To say my military aspirations were going well would be an understatement. I went to SLC, a somewhat shy, nervous boy and returned home in August a confident, happy, and focused teenager. At Borden, we lived in a barracks with eight other cadets per room, from all across Canada. Despite being at my height of sexuality, sex with others never seemed to cross my mind, perhaps because I still had no real idea of what it meant. My roommates were all great guys and we became a great team. The Senior Leaders Course taught cadets instructional technique, drill, effective speaking, and a variety of sports. My flight won the top athlete's award and I scored the Mutual Drill Trophy at the graduation parade. It

MCpl Mike Gariepy. (Author's Photo)

seemed like anything I touched in the military, I excelled in. That's probably because I loved it. My drill instructor was a Regular Force military policeman named MCpl Mike Gariepy. It wasn't unusual, Borden was a large Regular Force training base, and the MP school was right there. He was the image of professionalism; always strict but fair, impartial, and highly trained for his secondary role as a drill instructor to cadets. I remember thinking that my father and MCpl Gariepy were somewhat the same, and thinking how he and my father shared so many values. That summer, I vowed to combine those two role models and pattern my style after them. I wanted to be a perfect military example, just like my father and my drill instructor.

In the fall of 1972, I was promoted so fast to Warrant Officer 1st Class (WO1), the top rank in the non-commissioned ranks, that I only got to wear the WO2 rank badges for a few weeks. I had made it to my first goal; I was the top Air Cadet in Cornwall. The next few years were heady times. I revelled in learning by experience how to lead an Air Cadet squadron as Squadron Warrant Officer. I got to learn how to fly gliders on weekends and got my glider license in Pendleton, Ontario, at the Gatineau Gliding Club. I undertook a short lived program and earned a Para Rescue badge in Air Cadets, completing seven parachute jumps at the Ottawa Skydiving Centre. I also learned standard First Aid. I was awarded the Strathcona Medal, the only medal afforded cadets in my time. In my role as senior cadet, I worked closely with a wonderful man, my first Commanding Officer, Major Robert Beauchemin CD. Maj. Beauchemin was an icon in Air Cadets in Cornwall, and was like a father to me. He always sought my opinion on matters pertaining to cadets and gave me a very wide berth in running the squadron. While authority was the norm in powerful CO and SWO positions at the time, Major Beauchemin taught me to lead with selflessness and compassion. He put everyone first, and taught me to do the same. Under his leadership the squadron flourished and I grew

Warrant Officer First Class Steven Deschamps at November 11 ceremonies in Cornwall, Ontario, circa 1973. (Author's Photo)

up thinking I wanted to be an officer like him.

I didn't know many gay people growing up. There was a guy a little older than me that lived on our street in Cornwall. His name was Larry. He was an only child, early in his teens, and had feminine mannerisms. At the time, he was mocked for his outlandishness; he was gay and

wasn't afraid to show it. I was too immature to recognize the true strength of character Larry displayed, instead, I was afraid of him. Larry was three to four years older, and none of the older boys on the street would play with him. Most played hockey, Larry preferred cutting women's hair. He was ostracized not because people got to know him, but because people were afraid to get to know him. I remember thinking how different he was from everyone else, and while I never got to know him much either, he made me insecure by just being himself. Being effeminate was the de jour way of coping if you were gay and it scared the hell out of me. While I struggled with understanding and accepting my sexuality, Larry was the visible symbol of the stereotype of the day. Today, we see queens as celebrated, witness the popularity of the TV show RuPaul's Drag Race. When I was young, you had to be courageous and campy if you wanted to survive coming out as gay. I was just not up to the challenge. Instead, I buried my head in denial, repressed any sexual desires, and focused on excelling at my love; the military lifestyle.

Summer times were always exciting for me when I was a teenager. When my school friends were having to spend their summers in what I thought were dreary jobs at the local McDonalds, I would get paid to teach cadets at summer camps in places like Trenton, Ontario and Cold Lake, Alberta. I would be flown on military aircraft to my job, not bicycle every morning to a dreary fast food place.

In 1974, my summer military job was to be on the leadership staff of the Senior Leaders Course, then in Cold Lake. It had moved from Borden to Cold Lake the year before, and somehow, the leadership academic portion had been lost in the move. I knew this because in 1972, when I was a cadet on course, the leadership tasking, and exercises were some of the best parts, and I had excelled in them. When I got to Cold Lake, Leadership was mostly teaching cadets map and compass skills. I thought, what happened here? Lost was the bush exercise with leadership practical tasking, classes in leadership styles, and the rest of what I had learned in Borden. With the CO's blessing, I set out to build a leadership package that would be the best of breed. To that end, I borrowed the Aide Memoire from the Canadian Forces Officer Candidate School, all the leadership material I could find in the various manuals, and over three summers formulated a new program to teach and assess leadership for cadets attending the Senior Leaders Course. The program was a huge success, and I learned that in the military, there was nothing I couldn't do. I had good help, I was able to attract brilliant minds, and together, we inspired each other!

Chapter 2

AN OFFICER & A GENTLEMAN

I turned eighteen in 1974, and was immediately enrolled in the RCAF Reserves as Cadet Instructor List Officer for 325 Air Cadet Squadron in Cornwall. In those days, because I was a Cadet WO1, I was enlisted as a second lieutenant and appointed as Training Officer for the squadron.

I remember putting on my uniform as an officer for the first time. The CAF had been unified into one service, so we all wore a green uniform, instead of the traditional blue Air Force colours. I was soon promoted to lieutenant and then captain and worked summers at CFB Cold Lake as the Officer in Charge of Leadership.

In my various duties as a Cadet Instructor List Officer, I played important roles as a part time reservist, almost always in training. During the winters I was Training Officer at a cadet survival training school at Lac Desmarais just outside of Mont Tremblant, north of Montreal. Cadets from all over Montreal would come to the decommissioned, rented monastery where we had the survival school, and spend freezing weekends learning how to survive in parachute teepees, etc. My boss was the charismatic Major Marcel Bineault. He had caught wind of my survival training and hired me to work weekends as the lead

Photo credit from my personal photo collection The Leadership Staff, Senior Leaders Course circa 1978. I'm in the centre with the tray I was given by my team. (Author's Collection)

training officer. We would have 150 or so cadets every weekend, training in weather that often got below -30°C. I remember demonstrations I did of how to cook bacon and eggs in paper bags over an old tomato juice can-converted stove using wax candles for a heat.

During the summer of 1975, I was a lieutenant and selected to co-lead a summer camp experience for sixteen cadets in Montreal. Our job was to mount a parade to ceremonially raise the flags at Man and His World, the site of the former Expo 67. I remember thinking how hard that summer was; I only worked for an hour in the morning and again in the evening, but keeping sixteen or so teenagers occupied and motivated proved to be a challenge and one of the hardest summers I remember working. The guy that came after me to head the same operation, became a great friend years later. To this day I appreciate ice cream even more thanks to Norman Comeau, retired Cdr, CIC Branch Advisor.

By the time September of 1976 rolled around, I had started studying Business Administration at St. Lawrence College in Cornwall. The three year program was part of my grand plan to join the Regular Force as an officer under the Direct Entry Plan. It's curious, even at twenty years of age, I had a foreboding about my future career in the Armed Forces. While my sexual experience was still extremely limited, I knew more and more I was gay. I rationalized that I could have joined the Armed Forces in 1976 under the ROTP program at eighteen years of age, and gone to military college. My crazy thinking, living a deep secret that I could not talk to anyone about, was that if I joined under the ROTP program, and went to military college, I would owe the military a nine year contract for paying for my education. I reasoned it was better to spend my own money, go to St. Lawrence College and get my own education, and join under the Direct Entry Program. That way, if things did not go well, I could quit anytime without owing the government any money. Funny how you think when you are young, ill informed and worried about how being gay might affect your life.

College was exciting. Going to school in Cornwall on a smaller campus was great. The late 70s were fun and college life was full of adventure and interesting people. I made some good friends that are still friends to this day.

It was also the time I started sexual experimentation as a gay guy. The college parties were always fun, and you never knew who you could meet. I was still popular with girls, but I couldn't get interested. Instead, trips by car to Montreal proved educational. The Montreal gay pub scene was just beginning in the late 70s, and Montreal had underground meeting bars and parks where gay people could meet others. I remember reading a story in the Montreal Gazette detailing the meetings of gays at La Fontaine Park. Who would know that La Fontaine Park would be the place where I met my first love, on a sunny afternoon in 1980.

OPP Constable Nick Deschamps, circa 1976. (Author's Collection)

Life never seemed to go easy for me though. While I was at the top of my personal life, tragedy would once again come to my family.

My oldest brother, Nick, had joined the Ontario Provincial Police when he was young, not too long after my father died. He was thirteen years older than me. Nick always tried to be my dad after our father had died. He was bright, articulate, and passionate about the things he loved. He loved being an OPP officer and was fortunate in being posted to the Lancaster detachment, not far from Cornwall. He had been a great hockey player, like my other brothers Bob and John, and could have played in the pros. He married at the age of twenty-three in 1966, young by today's standards.

On March 17, 1977 the Cornwall Standard Freeholder newspaper had a front page story that hit close to home: "OPP Officer Found Shot." At first, the earliest reports the public could get were that this charismatic young hockey playing OPP officer was found just outside his jurisdiction at first dawn, in his cruiser, with the engine still running. The farmer that found my brother Nick on the side road leading to his property, said the window was shot out and the constable was in the driver's seat, a gunshot wound to the head. The OPP had already contacted us; the initial investigation showed all the signs of a suicide. As is the case today, police officers are one of the professions with the highest suicide rates.

Nick had been in trouble before his death; rumours of extra-marital relations had resulted in a recent divorce. The OPP had threatened a transfer to the north of Ontario, and things sunk so far into despair that my brother felt that the only way out was to commit suicide. I was twenty-one. You have no idea what it is like to lose a brother to suicide. Even today, I still run between grief and rage thinking about his death. But as much as a brother can feel loss, the worst was watching our mother bury her son. There is no grief greater than a parent losing a child, of that I am sure.

For me, I found myself back at the Cornwall Funeral Home, in the same room where my father had laid, seven years earlier. To this day, I still get horrible feelings when I smell flowers like you find at funerals and I rarely attend wakes.

Life never returned to normal after my brother's funeral. I remember feeling empty and confused, but not able to do anything about it. So, like when my father had died, I buried myself in my studies and my military life and tried to forget the pain.

Time flew fast. I was working on my plan: complete my three year Business Administration diploma and join the Regular Force as a pilot.

In 1977, I was the editor of the St. Lawrence College newspaper Echoes. I had taken on the job because the paper was failing, and I thought I could make it better. I set about recruiting my friends to work on the paper, and together we got the tabloid back into the black, and I was able to give other students a stipend for writing articles. The paper had a modest office in the new wing of the college, beside the guidance counsellor's office. It was a great place to hang out, and people were always stopping in. On weekends, I had keys to get into the college so it often proved a place where I could be found alone, doing projects or working on papers.

It was in that office that I met "Jim Crawley", or so he told me his name was. What I am about to describe is beyond understanding. But it happened. I was only able to piece together the significance of this unfortunate meeting much later in life, not until 2018 did I realize how impactful Jim Crawley had been on the rest of my life.

The anonymous letter you will read about later was always a mystery to me recalling later events. It wasn't until 2018, I made peace with the concept that only the military intelligence community could pull off the likes of what you will read about shortly.

Chapter 3

THE BEGINNING OF THE END

In the fall of 1978, I was beginning my second year of college and was the new Editor-in-Chief of Echoes, the college newspaper. It was a warm and sunny fall and life was especially good. My marks were above average, I enjoyed my studies, and my reserve cadet military career was paying my college bills. My mom let me live at home, so expenses were little, and the beer flowed freely at the local pubs, where students and professors often met after school.

My fellow students were all in their late teens or early twenties. There was an Arts professor who hung around with two gay twin students who were always attracting attention, not only for their good looks, but the outlandish rumours of parties and orgies at local homes on weekends. I was too chicken to accept invitations.

Within the first weeks of the fall of 1978, a funny looking guy started showing up on campus. He was in his mid thirties, and had a short US marine style haircut which, for the 70s, was very rare for a civilian. We could never figure out if he was a student or a professor, but took note of his strange appearance and the fact that no one seemed to know him. His name was Jim Crawley.

One day, Jim appeared at my newspaper office door and introduced himself. I was paying students $10 per article that they wrote for the newspaper, a lot of money in those days. His initial pretence was that he wanted to write for us. During our first meeting, he started dropping hints that he knew some of my military friends from my summer experiences at Cold Lake. He seemed to know of my comings and goings in military circles very well, and tried to become my military buddy. He told me he was with the US Army on loan to Canada's intelligence community and that we had lots in common. He was alway vague, and frankly, I wrote him off as nuts.

It was not long after our first meeting that he stopped back in again, this time showing me records of names of my fellow students who had taken books out from various local libraries on communist subjects. The books were mainstream: Lenin, Stalin, and other communist-themed type books. The type you might take out researching papers at school. The list was long and I wondered how he managed to get it, or for that matter why. In 1978, there was no internet, there was no cell phone, you did things the hard way. You physically had to do the work.

He soon told me that his job was to identify communist sympathizers and wanted me to help him. Now I knew he was loony! In any case, he planned to meet with me off campus later in the week, where he said he would explain everything. I remember agreeing to meet with him, and suddenly getting a cold chill down my spine. Later that Friday, I stopped into the office next door and had coffee with the college placement officer and asked if he knew who this Crawley guy was. No one knew anything about him.

On the weekend, I went into the college newspaper office. My office was in the new wing of the campus, and was locked on weekends. I had keys both to the building and the office. That Sunday, I found a yellow manilla envelope stuffed under my office door. It was dated the day before. To my shock and

Government Gouvernement of Canada du Canada	MEMORANDUM	NOTE DE SERVICE

		SECURITY CLASSIFICATION - DE SÉCURITÉ
TO à	SP Deschamps	UNCLASS
		OUR FILE - NÒ RÉFÉRENCE
	CORNWALL, ONTARIO	78-155o49MJ
		YOUR FILE V/RÉFÉRENCE
FROM DE	Major D. 'Jim' Crawley	
	Asst. DD-SPD	DATE
	ILO(DND/MCC) OTTAWA' ONTARIO	18.11.78

SUBJECT
OBJET "Loose Lips Sink Ships"

It is important to me that I have the opportunity to sit and chat with you in private on Wednesday. I should think that in the meantime it would be in your best interests and in my best interests that conversation in advance of this chat relating to the possible content of that conversation be restricted completely. (I do not include ~~----~~ ~~----~~ here).

While I am surprised how quickly news travels at your school (i.e. Mr. Richter at the Student Placement Office), I hope that this has been the extent of it. I must also ask you to respect the above conversational restriction with family and friends, buddies in the Highlanders or any other associates in Military or civilian positions.

You are of course free to do as you wish in this matter. In any event, you are quite welcome to do as you please after having talked with me on Wednesday.

To prevent matters from going out of proportion here, I might mention at this point that I am concerned only with matters relating to past Senior Leaders Courses and similar topics which will assist me in the preparation of a personal paper on the effectiveness and productivity of such summer-time activities. It is - I must stress - purely a personal enquiry and not related to existing SL programs in formation at this point in time.

So, we are talking about things which are more personal than official in nature. In addition to which, as long as you remain a civilian I do not have any power or jurisdiction over your actions, I merely happened to be here in Cornwall and realized that I was in the vicinity of a friend of young Burniston and thought I would drop in for a 'hello'.

I will stop by later today on my return from Ottawa to see if you have received this note. If I do not drop by, then I shall see you on Wednesday at 1500 hours.

Don't work to hard. Best regards.

D.'Jim' Crawley
MAJOR
Asst. DD-SPD
ILO(DND/MCC) OTTAWA, Ont.

TPH:mb

This document is copy of the original given to me.

surprise, it was from Major Jim Crawley. Asst. DD-SPD ILO (DND/MCC), whatever that was. I read the letter as threatening. DD-SPD? Those were my initials. He had my social insurance number! How did he get that? He didn't like that I was asking about him on campus, and made veiled threats that held no power over me as long as I remained a civilian.

The letter was on Canadian Government Memorandum paper, current for that period of time. Why a Major in intelligence wanted me to keep quiet while he was inquiring about the effectiveness of summer employment at military camps for a personal paper was simply bogus in my mind. I was keen enough to notice that the bottom lower left of his memo had the standard typist letters used in those days, of the author and typist initials. TPH:mb. So whomever dictated this typed memo had initials TPH, not DJC as in D. Jim Crawley whom the memo was supposed to be from.

I got more and more nervous during the coming days in anticipation of the Wednesday meeting at 3pm at a local pizza restaurant. I started telling a few close friends of my upcoming meeting and warned them, out of sheer fear, to call the police and tell them this story if I suddenly disappeared after the Wednesday meeting. I had no idea what to do.

That Wednesday, I met Jim Crawley at the local pizza restaurant he had chosen. He walked in wearing an ill-fitting, mismatched suit jacket and slacks, and looked completely out of place. I remember thinking he had the size and face, glasses and thin moustache that made him look like Heinrich Himmler. He sat down and started telling me his story. He was a US Army Major working in intelligence, seconded to the Canadian Department of National Defence (DND). He needed my cooperation, and anyone else I could enlist, to research, identify, and document known communist sympathizers or agents we could find on campus.

It was to be a secret operation and I was to tell no one. He trusted me because I was young and had a stellar military record in cadets and reserves. He stressed how important this mission was. I was flabbergasted. I felt I was in a trap and that this guy was someone right out of the McCarthy era, and was probably nuts. Needless to say I wanted no part of this.

It's not often that one can look back and think their instincts were right on, but this was one of those occasions.

Intuitively, I looked at Jim Crawley and told him I wanted proof of his credentials. I asked him to produce his ID card for me. He refused and laughed that a senior officer would have to identify himself to a junior officer. I told him I wanted him to produce a letter from his superiors to prove this operation was legitimate. He told me he would not do that. I told him that I would go to the local police and call the military police in Ottawa. He laughed again and dared me too. He said they would know nothing and would be prevented from investigating.

Then, that moment of inspiration set in: I told him if he did not produce the documents I wanted I would go to the local Member of Parliament, Ed Lumley and tell him this story. Ed Lumley was a prominent local Member of Parliament and Minister of Tourism in Pierre Elliot Trudeau's (PET) cabinet. I told Crawley I had friends who were related to Minister Lumley and had easy access to him. Crawley blanched. I didn't realize it at the time, but PET was no fan of the Canadian military, and Crawley seemed to know that.

Crawley started stumbling for words. He grew annoyed and aggravated and for the first time, I noticed fear. Crawley told me if I did that, I would blow months of intelligence gathering, countless man hours of research, and jeopardize this major operation and his career. I stuck to my guns and my terms. Crawley quickly brought the meeting to an end, in a furor. As he left, he gave me that defeated, contemptuous look you sometimes see in the movies when the guilty sentence is pronounced on the bad guy.

I went back to campus and joined some friends for a beer, recalling the entire story to a few of them. We laughed it off, thinking Crawley was some kind of nut, and drank enough beer that afternoon to put the story to bed in our minds. I always kept the original copy and the manila envelope of the letter I got from Major D. Jim Crawley.

Who would have thought that forty years later, that letter would shed some light on events that haunted me for years. Who wrote the anonymous letter? With secret files from the SIU investigation provided to me later, it was determined the letter was written by an adult who knew how to write in military style. The SIU concluded it was not written by a cadet; so who was left?

I graduated from my three year college diploma program from St. Lawrence College in the spring of 1979. Now, I had all the credentials needed to apply for the Canadian Armed Forces Regular Force as a Direct Entry Officer.

My last summer employment as a reserve captain was to be the Air Instructor at a new Cadet Instructor List training school in Edmonton, at what was then CFB Edmonton Griesbach Barracks. I was to drive my car out to Edmonton that summer. Working in Alberta was a great last hurrah for me as a reserve officer before enlisting in the Regular Force. It was a great summer. In July, I walked into the Canadian Forces Recruiting Centre in Edmonton, in uniform as a captain, and I remember the sergeant asked me what he could do for me, "sir". I replied, "I want to join up."

I was young, healthy, had a stellar record of cadets and reserve force service, and I was bilingual. It took no time to process my application in Edmonton while I continued my reserve military employment on the Base. Soon, I was off to Toronto for a week during the summer to attend Aircrew Selection at DCIEM, the Defence and Civil Institute of Environmental Medicine. That week consisted of a battery of physiological and aptitude testing to determine if I was a candidate for pilot training in the Air Force. Shortly after that, I returned to Edmonton to finish my summer employment and I drove back to Cornwall in August on a high! I had a great summer helping to set up a new reserve officer training school, I loved teaching, and my future career dreams had been initiated. I had started enrolment in the CAF.

I no sooner got home to Cornwall from Edmonton when I got the call from the recruiting centre in Ottawa. I had been accepted as a pilot trainee, and I was to go to Ottawa, complete the paperwork, and swear the oath. I was to report to the Canadian Forces Officer Candidate School (CFOCS) in Chilliwack, British Columbia on the long weekend of September 1979. If there was ever a time I think I was the happiest in my life, it was on that drive to Chilliwack, a newly minted officer candidate in the CAF.

Chapter 4

THE BEGINNING OF MY RCAF CAREER

The fall of 1979 in British Columbia was beautiful. I remember thinking how extraordinary the weather and the geography was. Even though I had fallen in love with the province at fifteen years of age as an Air Cadet; I had been selected to take the Outward Bound Mountain School Leadership course in Keremeos, I could not get enough of such a beautiful province.

The Canadian Forces Officer Candidate School course is a boot camp for new officers. There were 300 or so on my serial from across Canada when I arrived, and because I was labelled francophone by the recruiting centres, I was loaded into a French platoon. Now make no mistake, I was bilingual, but I remember thinking that if I had my choice, I would rather do this course in English. I dreaded trying to do exams in French, as always, a very difficult language to read and write in. I asked to be moved to an English platoon. The interview with my Company Commander, a Royal 22 Regiment major went well. I remember him telling me that he thought it was courageous that I would be willing to take the course in my second official language, English, and he wished me well. I was transferred in

C Company 13 Platoon, my platoon chums after a run. I'm the tall one, fourth from top right. (Author's Collection)

my first days to Charlie Company, and as fate would have it, transferred to the first platoon of female nursing officers to go through CFOCS. Of the thirty or so candidates in my platoon, only six of us were male; one a nursing candidate officer, and the others a mixed batch of military occupations.

I arrived at CFOCS having been groomed with years of cadet and officer training. While I had no idea of the challenges, I easily understood the methodology. In years prior, I had taught many of the same classes. I breezed through training without breaking a sweat. When leadership tasks were assigned in the field to challenge our abilities, I was always selected by the candidate being assessed as their second in command (2ic) to be a resource on how to help through the task.

My platoon mates were mostly nurses by training, so if I got even a sniffle, they were all over me, nursing me back to health, for fear of losing a powerful, walking embodiment of what to

2 Lt Deschamps, top candidate, serial 7907 CFOCS. (Author's Collection)

do on course. At night, I taught classes to my platoon mates going over military law, orders, traditions etc, in exchange for them helping with pressing my shirts while I gave the class. Boot bashes were regular: I was the centre of our platoon activity for my platoon mates and I loved it.

By the time the course was over, I was selected Top Candidate of the course and commanded the graduation parade. For anyone else, commanding a ceremonial parade of three companies, through a very precise order barking command, in both official languages, would have been harrowing but I barely broke a sweat. On the day of the final graduation parade, we were ordered to wear the ranks we were being paid at. Although an officer candidate on course, at the rank of Officer Cadet, non-commissioned, because I was a Direct Entry Officer, I commanded the parade as a Second Lieutenant. The School Regimental Sergeant Major came marching to me directly on completion of the parade, I remember thinking, "Oh my god, what did I screw up?" He stopped short, saluted me for the first time in my Regular Force career, and asked for a dollar bill, the traditional offering for your "first salute."

Now you have to be wondering, this is all nice…but you're twenty-three years of age! You must have known you were gay by now?

Indeed, how smart on your part!

In Chilliwack, being on a course with mostly girls, in a military school dominated by males, I must have been in my glory! Not quite. Let me explain.

At twenty-three, I was no longer in doubt I was gay. I had trained myself how not to show any outward mannerisms or show tell-tale signs I was gay. I was certifiably crazy in my own mind. I suffered from internalized homophobia: the fear of being identified as gay. And I had every right to be: if the people around me in my chosen career thought I was gay, there would be swift and dire consequences! And yet, I went through officer candidate school unscathed. Aircrew selection, in all its scientific approach to determine if I would be a good pilot, didn't determine I was gay. No one suspected. The few weekends we had leave, I would drive off alone to Vancouver, an hour drive from Chilliwack, stay at a hotel in the west end, and indulge my fantasies. By Sunday afternoon, I was driving back to Base Chilliwack with no one the wiser. In 1979, Vancouver was a gay man's dream: gay clubs, gay cruising places, even a boys town on Davie Street where young gay guys hung out. I could keep my secret, play

2Lt Steven Deschamps on OJT at 10 Tactical Air Group, CFB St-Hubert, 1980. (Author's Collection)

out my young man's desires, and keep a career in a homophobic workplace and no one was the wiser. Or so I thought.

The fall of 1979 went by too fast. In December, I graduated at the top of my class and was ordered to 10 Tactical Air Group HQ in Montreal to commence on the job training as assistant to the Group Flight Safety Officer.

Montreal! Are you kidding? How could it get any better? I remember thinking how wonderful life was. I was doing what I loved. I proved to myself I could keep my gay world secret, known only to myself and my consorts, and my employer, the Canadian Armed Forces, the most homophobic employer of the time, was none the wiser. Life was too good!

In Montreal, as a second lieutenant living in officer quarters, life was good. My job was on the job training or OJT. In other words, until a place opened up at flying school, I would be paid, housed, clothed, and fed by her Majesty's Armed Forces, in a life of bliss, with no defined job. Sure I was given tasks, largely to keep me out of the way of the pilots that surrounded me. Mine was in flight safety. I remember pouring over the many highly documented investigations of Air Force aircraft accidents. It was all fascinating for me. Pilots are not known for their administrative skills, so the pilots attached to St-Hubert's 10 TAG HQ took pity on the bright articulate 2Lt Deschamps OJT in Flight Safety. When they went flying, as they had to do because they were in designated pilot positions and had to remain current, they would often ask me to go for the ride. I got to go co-pilot in CF-5 jet fighters, Otters, Twin Hueys, Kiowa's etc. I never refused a ride.

It was then I experienced my first professional death of friends: two guys I had flown with often, had been tasked to pick up one of the first Chinook twin bladed transport helicopters the government had recently bought. I was asked to go for the ride with them on the trip from Montreal to Elmira, New York and return. Other duties stopped me from going. On their trip back in the first Chinook, flying back to Montreal, the rotors went out of sync at altitude and tore the aircraft apart in mid air. My two friends perished in the crash. It was my first experience dealing with the loss of comrades, friends, dying for what they loved. It was not the last. I think it is still why, regardless of whether I am ordered, or not, I still go to the cenotaph closest to me on November 11 to stop and remember. I have done this, without a missed year, since I was thirteen years old.

It was in Montreal, in the spring of 1980, that I had my first romance. I met Denis one spring Sunday afternoon, in La Fontaine Park in Montreal. The internet was not around yet and gay bars were only starting to surface, the only way to meet anyone gay was to go to the local cruising place, which, for Montreal at that time, was La Fontaine Park.

Denis and I became quick partners. He still lived with his parents in the north end of Montreal and I was living in St-Hubert, in officer quarters. Denis was completely out to his family, and they quickly adopted me as one of their own. With Denis, I often stayed in his bedroom with him at his family home. I was always so envious how Denis was surrounded by a family he did not have to hide his sexuality from. After my father had died, the wind had been taken out of my family life. It's like we didn't know how to relate to each other; each of us were off doing our own thing, and there was little family life. After my brother Nick died, I knew, or thought I knew, that our family unit was too fragile to support another tragedy like me coming out, so I just stayed in my closet learning how not to betray my secret to them.

The bliss of being in love was soon to be tested. My orders were to be posted to 3 Canadian Forces Flying Training School in Portage la Prairie, Manitoba. I was to report on April 23, 1980. Denis and I spent all our time together right up until I packed the car and started the drive from Montreal to Portage la Prairie. I think we all know what it's like to go through your first love, and having to pick up and leave Montreal was heartbreaking. We did not want to break up, I could not bring Denis with me for obvious reasons, and I did not want to leave the Armed Forces. We embarked on a long distance love affair. However, in 1980, there were no cell phones, in fact, land lines, and telephone booth long distance calls were rare and very expensive. There was no text messaging, no internet, just loneliness and the post office.

The CT 134 Musketeer, the primary training aircraft at 3 CFFTS. (Author's Collection)

I arrived at Portage la Prairie and tried to make the best of it. Unlike any military training I had up to that point, 3 CFFTS approach to life seemed like a cutting school. About a hundred of us arrived to start pilot training on the Musketeer that spring in May. Within weeks, a dozen were cut and the numbers dropped without rhyme or reason.

I remember seeing a fellow pilot candidate, having a beer after flying, in the officer mess wearing our tan fly suits and he was wearing an earring in one ear. I never saw him again after that evening. People would disappear, "ceased training" was the term used. If you were CT, you disappeared. The practice was to get the candidate off the base quickly. You never got to say goodbye.

I was miserable. Portage la Prairie is in the middle of nowhere in Manitoba. It is a community of less than a few thousand supporting the flying school. The only reprieve from life was the odd weekend where I could go to Winnipeg, a one hour drive away. I was feeling the separation from Denis, lacked motivation, and could not concentrate. Denis would join me when he could. My instructor provided very little feedback; the school existed to see if you could learn quickly and if you had aptitude for pilot skills. The idea was to cut the weeds out, and send the best to Moose Jaw where you would really learn how to fly.

And to make things worse for me, I could not tell anyone why I was miserable. I was separated from my first love, isolated in the prairies, and going through all the love pangs a young man goes through when they first fall in love, but for me, I had to make sure no one knew. The very odd time I could talk to Denis, I had to be discreet and call from a telephone booth on base. I had to make sure the tears in my eyes and the emotional disposition did not follow me back to the barracks for fear of having to explain to my fellow classmates. This went on for a few weeks. While I liked my training, I could not get past the separation anxieties and the huge stress of being away from the one I loved. Perhaps it is not unlike those brave soldiers that left their loved ones and went off to war. It sure felt like that for me. The big difference, I rationalized, was that my existence in its present state, was untenable. I could not keep this up for much longer.

My life was in despair. I was under tremendous pressure to memorize long checklists by heart, and be able to execute them flawlessly to show my instructors I knew what to do instinctively if there was an emergency on board my aircraft. All this in addition to learning how to fly a new plane. I was not sleeping well, and the pressures were mounting. I had to make a decision.

It took me about three weeks of flying training at Portage to realize I could not go through it. I decided to withdraw from flying training and hoped that somehow, some way, my military career and my secret love life could be reconciled.

I wrote a memo to my Squadron Commander requesting release from flying duties. The reply was quick and shocking. Despite the fact that I thought I was failing miserably, I was informed that I was actually doing very well. I had above average flying marks, and average marks on ground school exams. I was shocked. In any case, I managed to convince the Squadron Commander that flying was not for me, knowing if I told him the real reasons, I would be doomed. What happened next took me by surprise.

The process involved an interview with a Personnel Selection Officer. The Canadian Armed Forces did not want to lose a bilingual, top officer candidate, and started looking for options. I was offered a transfer to public affairs where, if I completed a six month selection process at NDHQ in Ottawa, I would be reclassified to be a public affairs officer in the Canadian Forces. "Perfect!" I thought. I looked up the posting opportunities for public affairs: they were only posted to big cities like Ottawa, Toronto, Halifax, Edmonton, and Victoria. I would be posted initially to Ottawa NDHQ which was only a two hour drive from Montreal where Denis still lived. I jumped at the opportunity.

I was to be moved to officers quarters at CFB Winnipeg awaiting disposition of my career. For the time being, the CAF had attached me to the Cadet HQ staff at CFB Winnipeg where I would be doing work at the HQ, for which I had a lot of experience. I was working with other officers who were class B reserves officers whose job it was to administer the cadet program in the Prairies. As a Regular Force second lieutenant, I had as much, and in some cases more, experience around the cadet program than they did. I did not work with cadets, in fact all of my work with the cadet program for the last years of my cadet instructor list reserve days before enrolling in the Regular Force was working with the adult officers of the cadet program.

I arrived in Ottawa in November of 1980 driving straight through to Montreal before reporting in, to be reunited with

Denis. I figured we would be able to figure things out, and that serving in Ottawa would be easier to hide my lifestyle given the size of the city.

And so I began my life as a Canadian Forces Public Affairs Officer.

Denis and I eventually got a place together in Vanier, a suburb of Ottawa, after I completed my initial acceptance into the PAFFO world which occurred in April 1981.

I worked for the Director of Exhibition and Displays. My boss was a long serving member, a sergeant, who was commissioned from the ranks of the photo trade and was now serving as a well-seasoned and very mellow Major. There were only four officers in the Directorate. Public Affairs in those days were very lean, only about thirty-five officers scattered across Canada, about twenty of us in various positions in Ottawa.

While I had immense regrets over losing out on a flying career in the Air Force, at least I was able to put my marketing training to work and help build and manage displays telling the world how good the Armed Forces of Canada were.

Life at home with Denis was nice, but cracks started to show early into our clandestine relationship. The toll a secret gay life took on two individuals in the early 80s is hard to describe. Our social life did not exist. I could not trust anyone to know our secret. Everyone knew us as "roommates." The most we got to do was to go back to Montreal on weekends and stay with Denis' family. Montreal had an exciting gay bar life and it was not unusual to go to bars and have celebrities like Ginette Reno, in her beginnings, do live performances. It was a fun life in Montreal for us, but returning to Ottawa to live in secret eventually took its toll. Denis and I split in the spring of 1981. He moved back to his parents' house, and I moved into Officer Quarters at Rockcliffe, or CFB Ottawa North as it was known then.

Chapter 5

THE START OF A DARK ERA

In the spring of 1981, I was closing in on twenty-five years old. I thought I had experienced lots: I had loved and lost, I was sacrificing a huge part of my life by hiding in the closet, making sure that no one knew I was gay, but my military career continued to inspire me. It did not matter that I was not flying, I was jet setting around Canada doing public relations for the Canadian Armed Forces. I was respected by my new bosses, all of which were in their fifties and loved that new blood had been injected into the system. My performance appraisal rocked and I was being fast tracked for promotion to Captain. I attended Supreme Headquarters Allied Powers Europe (SHAPE) in Mons, Belgium to take the International Public Affairs course. I was to be loaded on a six month US Defence Information School course in Indiana to learn the craft of military public affairs and I was sent to Gagetown, New Brunswick in 1981 for RendezVous 81, a Canadian army divisional exercise supported by my old friends in the Air Force from 10 TAG.

My job was to tell the Air Force's story on the exercise. I was in on the daily briefings of the brigadier-general commanding and had access, as a junior lieutenant, to all the brass. I loved it. So much so, the army got pissed off because all the news coming out of Gagetown that summer seemed to be about the small air resources attached from Montreal and Bagotville. I proved I was an adept storyteller, knew the media and the press well, and they knew me.

Now, one could think that this is a fairy tale story of the life of an aviator who loved his work and was good at it.

That might have happened if it was not for that fateful day my boss stepped into my office in April 1982, to tell me that I had a routine security clearance interview with a sergeant, Military Police, at SIU in Rockcliffe the following week. I had never heard of the SIU (Special Investigative Units). Turns out, not many had. They existed as plain clothes military police investigators who, I was told, did all the major undercover work for military investigations, including the security clearance process. I was told it was routine and thought nothing of it.

What I am about to tell you all happened. Much of what I tell you here now, I reconstruct from the classified files I received in 2018 from the Government of Canada as part of class action suit settlement agreement.

Building where the SIU interrogation took place at CFB Ottawa North circa 1992 (Author's Collection)

I arrived at CFB Ottawa North at the appointed time, in uniform, to the old Photo Building, and an obscure side door of the building with no number above it to be greeted by two SIU sergeants in plain clothes. I had never heard of the SIU and did not understand why they were not in uniform. I only saw these two individuals who introduced themselves by producing business cards. I was ushered into a small soundproof room, with one table, a hanging light without shades, and walls that were covered in what appeared to be egg cartons for soundproofing. It was an interrogation room. The two sergeants sat with a large folder in front of them and began asking routine questions. Where was I posted before Ottawa? Where had I lived? What were my hobbies? Who were my friends? After what seemed like a long period of time and dozens of questions about my life, they produced a letter, unsigned, typed in what appeared to be official DND style. It purported that in Winnipeg, I made sexual advances to an unnamed cadet. They asked me if I was gay. I denied making any sexual approaches to any cadet. In fact, when I was in Winnipeg I worked with the Cadet HQ on the Base and never saw any cadets. They then produced CF 100 Leave Request forms from Portage La Prairie from when I was posted there. On many of the forms I had faked addresses because I didn't want anyone to know that I was staying at a downtown Winnipeg hotel, visiting with my boyfriend Denis. I'm not sure why I lied about where I was staying, but then, I reasoned that the less the CAF really knew about me, the better. They used the faked address to build a case that I was lying and that I was gay. They asked if I had gone to certain gay bars in the Hull and Ottawa area, various hotels that were known to be gay hangouts. They asked if I knew other gay military members and showed me pictures of various other people. I told them I was young and that I was "experimenting" with guys. Eventually, I realized I could not hide my sexuality and told them I was gay. I realized years later that they needed a person to admit they were gay in order to proceed with CFAO 19-20. Admitting you were gay was the reason for the interrogations, otherwise, they had no way of proving anything. They experimented with the "Fruit Machine," a device invented by a Carleton University professor for the military, but it failed miserably.

The SIU made me a deal because they "felt sympathetic to me" and that I had a stellar rising career in the military.

They asked me to take a polygraph that would refute me being compromised or blackmailed by foreign agents. I agreed, provided they would ask me questions to refute the pedophile insinuations made in the anonymous letter. They agreed. The reasoning used in those days was that gays kept their sexuality secret and therefore were subject to blackmail and infiltration by foreign governments. History shows that great lies are used by Governments to cover the true intent of operations, and along the way, we have all paid a terrible price for our complacency.

The two sergeants told me that I was not to discuss their investigations or questions with anyone or I would be charged under the Official Secrets Act, and I was warned to not even talk to a priest.

When I was posted to Ottawa from Winnipeg, I had enough time in rank for promotion to lieutenant, however that did not occur. This was a period in time where a gay friend in Winnipeg warned me not to use phones to call him and that we were being followed. I dismissed the notion thinking he was given to exaggeration. Curiously, I remember hearing telltale clicks on my private phone line in my room in the barracks. I didn't realize it, but they were tapping my phone.

I was denied an automatic promotion, and I was finally promoted to lieutenant only after I had written a very sound memo quoting regulations. I believed my promotion was interfered with by the SIU at the time.

Around the same time, I was advised that I was going to be posted to Indiana for three months to take the US Public Affairs Officer course, a normal pre-requisite for career training and promotion to captain. I remember seeing the posting messages with dates and my names on it. Then the SIU interview occurred and my name was removed from the course. I was denied career progression training.

After the initial SIU interview, my peers at work started asking why I was being questioned by the SIU. They often did this over coffee in the lunchroom. My CO appeared very uncomfortable.

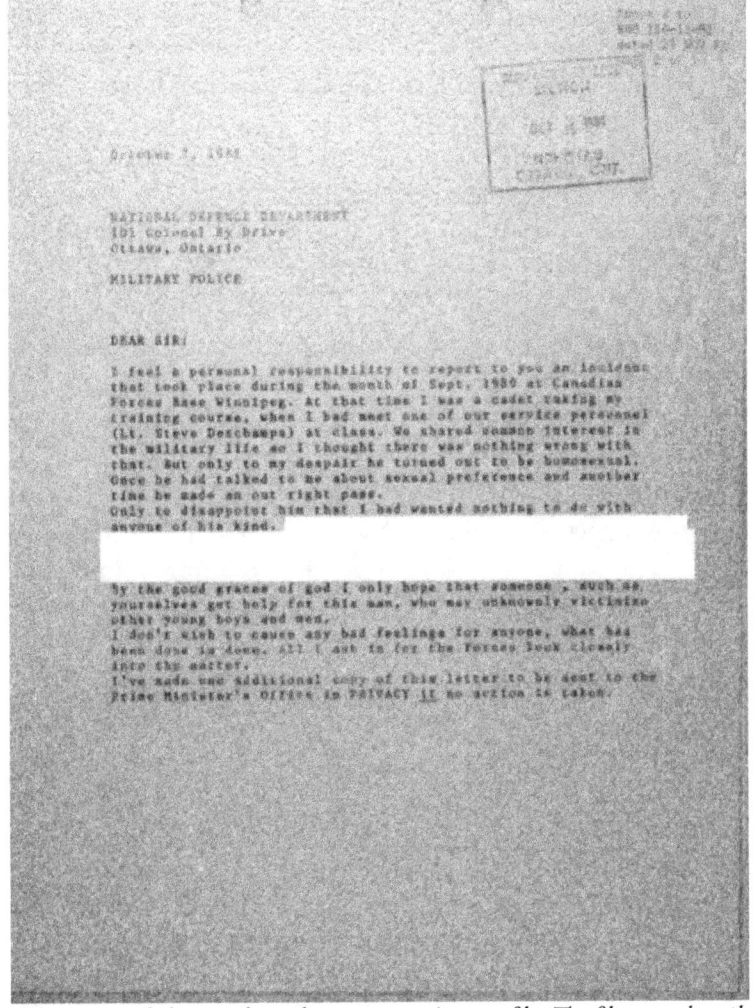

A letter provided to me from the government's secret files The files were heavily redacted by the Government before they were sent to me. (Author's Collection)

I wondered how these captains knew I had been interrogated? Innuendo soon came: "Only fags get interviewed by the SIU."

During the interview, the two sergeants asked many of the same questions over the course of about four to five hours. They would zero in on leave I had taken in Winnipeg and ask where I had been during my leave, where I had stayed, what time of day did I go to bed, who did I see, where did I eat. They would ask if I had been to dozens of different places, places I had no idea where they were or what existed there. They asked if I had sex with men, what kind of sex I preferred, top or bottom, what I preferred doing with women in bed, how long would a sex session last, who were my sexual contacts.

I was denied the right to have legal representation, denied the right to have a lawyer, denied all rights afforded today under our laws.

The irony of it all is that at roughly the same time I was being wrongly interrogated at CFB Ottawa, Her Majesty Queen Elizabeth II and Prime Minister Pierre Elliot Trudeau were signing the Charter of Rights and Freedoms on Parliament Hill in Ottawa.

I was requested to take a polygraph. This occurred in Ottawa again in the same area at CFB Rockcliffe at another time, days later. The person who did the polygraph was new to me. I don't remember being asked questions like if I was gay or if I had sex with men, but rather if I had given secrets away to foreign powers, along with more neutral questions like "Is today Wednesday?"

During the polygraph I was guarded and nervous. The polygraph was done with just the two of us in a small room that was very hot and the machines made stressful noises. The polygraph operator was unfriendly, uncaring, and distant.

He asked questions in a systematic manner, and on any question that seemed pertinent to their interests, he would lean over and make marks on the polygraph paper which stressed me even more.

In the interrogations, I was threatened with Official Secrets charges and jail time, if I was to tell anyone about the investigations or share any details. I was also threatened that if I did not cooperate with the questioning, they would use tactics like taking away my NDHQ ID pass, which meant I could not physically get into my workplace. That would make me Absent Without Leave or AWOL, or so they threatened, and that I could go to jail in Club Ed, the military prison in Edmonton, for up to two years. Because the SIU knew I lived in the officers quarters at the time of the interrogations, they threatened that if I did not answer the questions with what they wanted to hear, they could have me removed from my room in the quarters and that I would have to move my furniture and things out to the street overnight. They boasted they could do whatever they wanted and they were above regulation or law. At one point I remember them saying they could have me sent to Inuvik, an isolated posting in the arctic, where "the only sex I could have is with polar bears."

After the interrogations by the SIU in Ottawa in the spring of 1982, weeks would pass before anything would happen. I was never advised by anyone what the dispositions of the interrogations had led to. I was sworn not to speak to anyone. It was a very angst-ridden time as I didn't know what was going to happen. They used the Official Secrets Act to isolate me and to ensure no one would know what they were doing. It is clear to me now, they knew what they were doing would not be well received by Canadians, so they used threats to keep me from telling anyone what was going on. Sadly, I came to know they did this with all of us.

After a number of weeks, I was told to present to the National Defence Medical Centre in Ottawa and was ordered to report to a lieutenant-colonel who was a psychiatrist.

The psychiatrist was a professional. He was disarming, genuine and sincere. He was the only face of human kindness that was offered during this horrible eight months. He asked me a number of questions pertaining to my sexuality. He showed me a thick, confidential file that he said was about me from the SIU and that he said he had never read. I remember him saying that he thought the SIU were a bunch of sick people. His disarming manner and genuine care made me confide my sexuality to him, which he said would be held in strictest secrecy, as doctor-patient privilege. I talked about my sexuality openly. After one to two hours, he asked me what I was going to do. I told him I felt that my career was over in the military, and that I would look to find another job. He thought I had a good handle on things and that I was remarkably well composed, all things given. He said he would report to the authorities that "I was not gay in the usual sense of the term." He said that would trip them up a bit, but they were going to release me so I best prepare for that. He did not offer any follow up.

No one ever followed up with my health, nor did anyone in the military seem to care. At the time of my release, I was a lieutenant working for the Director of Exhibition and Displays (DXD) in Ottawa. The next I remembered I was ordered to appear on April 1, 1982 before the brigadier-general, the Director General Information, and head of our group at the NDHQ 101 Colonel By building. This was very intimidating to a lieutenant. He and I were alone for the fifteen minute meeting. He was aloof and arrogant. He stated to me that I would be released from the CAF because I was a threat to security and that my activity brought discredit to his unit. He made out that he was doing me a favour and that he negotiated my release as an honourable release instead of dishonourable, and that I should be grateful. This interview occurred in his office at NDHQ 101 Col By Drive. I asked that I be released under section 4C, volunteer release, in order not to have any employment repercussions. He agreed. The meeting was over. He did not shake my hand.

When it was determined I was going to be released, and it was public, I had got another job very quickly outside of the military and I tried to hide the fact that I was being released, telling people I decided to quit and get a better job.

I had found a job at Algonquin College in their public relations office. The salary I would make was more than I was making in the CAF. I used that as the pretext to my family and friends to hide the fact I was being released and was gay. I was to go to the NDHQ building on Col By Drive on June 9, 1982 for the final return of my ID, and sign the final papers. I was told not to report to my normal office that day but rather, at the appointed time to go to NDHQ. I would be on leave until July when I was to start my new job. I was escorted into the Commandant of NDHQ Administrative Unit, a full colonel, to sign the final papers. It was very intimidating. I could tell that everybody in the Orderly Room was watching me, like parading a criminal to jail. The Commandant showed me the final papers to sign after being paraded to finance, release, and security sections. I noted to the Commandant that I had negotiated a 4C release but that I was being documented out as 5D, "no longer advantageously employable." I told him I would not sign until it was corrected. The Commandant appeared agitated. He went to another office to make a call to the Brigadier-General. He returned after what seemed a long period and announced that the general was not available, and that if I did not sign today on the terms of the papers, I would not be released, and that I would still be in the military and could not report to my new job. He blackmailed me into signing the papers in front of him. I signed the final document in his office at NDHQ Orderly Room, a member of his staff escorted me to the street entrance, and I was booted out of the military to the street. I remember feeling like throwing myself off the Rideau bridge in front of me, but thought it was not high enough to kill me and no one would know why I died.

Later in life, from the unsealed documents I was provided as part of the settlement agreement of the class action suit, I noted that my brigadier-general had argued that because I was not provided with counsel, a 5D release could be challenged by me. Even then, they knew what they were doing was immoral, if not illegal.

I had to move out of quarters. My friends in quarters did not understand why I was leaving because I loved the military so much. I moved my belongings myself to an apartment on Bronson Street in Ottawa. All of my actions around this time were organized by me so as not to reveal what really happened to me. It was not for the fear of prosecution for breaking the Official Secrets Act, but more because I had to cope with the fact that my lifelong career was ending around me, in disgrace, unable to tell anyone about my sexuality and not knowing who I could talk to. I did not tell anyone, family or friends, for years after. Thus began a lifelong process of repressing everything I was and what happened to me, for what I believed was my own preservation.

I began telling white lies to hide my truths, a process I continued for many years. I still have problems admitting I'm gay. I had always known, or heard there was a risk in being a homosexual in the CAF at the time I enrolled. I had kept my sexuality secret. I never made friends with other gay guys and avoided at all costs knowing any other gay people in the military. I did not want to be put in the position of having to choose between being loyal to my friends or to my oath made in becoming an officer of honesty, loyalty, and courage.

At the time of my release, I knew I was discharged solely for being gay, but I had no idea it was part of a larger action or purge. I only learned later of the extent of the systematic purge of the CAF and RCMP of gays. I had no idea, in my arrogance perhaps, that I was purged as part of a concerted effort. I could not bring myself to think we Canadians could do that. I am still troubled immensely by it.

Chapter 6

THE FALLOUT

I am now only coming to realize what harm has occurred to me as a result of the Purge. I loved the military. I believe that if I had not been caught up in the Purge, I would have stayed in the military, retired as a senior officer, and had a completely different life. Over time, as acceptance of gay members became commonplace, I thought to myself how my life might have been so different if the Purge had not caught up to me.

I remember feeling bewildered watching CF members in uniform marching in the Gay Pride Parade in Vancouver and Victoria in the early 2010s. These events were always gut wrenching for me. Before 1982, I was private about my sexuality in order to be a CAF officer. When I was purged, despite my best abilities, and concerted efforts to put myself back together, I suffered an altered life because of the trauma. I still believe I am incapable of relationships. I have not had a meaningful relationship with anyone for more than a few months since the Purge. I do not trust anyone, and am cynical of people's motives. I still cannot find love within myself, for myself. I believe this is because I was robbed of that ability when I was purged.

When I was released, and no longer worried about the military finding out about my sexuality, I became addicted to sex. It became a full time, debilitating addiction. I had to move jobs frequently for fear, in my mind, that my employer would find out about my homosexuality and I would get fired again. I suffered from debilitating depressive symptoms. I have been treated for depression and have seen a psychiatrist to treat it. Invariably, antidepressants were prescribed off and on.

In 1992, when I was diagnosed with HIV, my doctor told me I would die within a few years, a very horrible death. In 1992 HIV was a death sentence as there was no known treatment. I was actually relieved! I thought, finally, this will all come to an end. I realized, at that point, that I could not escape death, and what the shame of dying of AIDS would bring to my family and friends.

I started down a path of revealing, in highly planned meetings, what my life had been like since being kicked out of the military, why I was kicked out of the military, and that I was gay. I was living in North Vancouver at the time, and I arranged for my mother to fly out to stay with me and then I would drive her back to Cornwall as a vacation trip together.

My motivation was in fact to tell my mother all the facts that she did not know, and by having her trapped in my car on a road trip for seven days with me driving would give me enough time and courage to tell her everything, and to manage her questions and angst.

I decided that as my final act of humanity, I would use all of my financial resources and strength left to redress the ignominious release that was proffered on me in 1982. I wanted to sue the government and hopefully, have my story told so that a change might occur. In consulting various people, I realized that I needed an actionable cause. At the time, statutes of limitation were against me. I was advised to re-enrol in the CAF, and when refused, I could sue as a Charter case.

Chapter 7

I'M COMING BACK!

I presented to the local Air Cadet squadron in North Vancouver in 1991, offering my services to the Commanding Officer, and was welcomed with open arms. I did not disclose that I was gay and my resume and course reports were highly redacted by me to hide my 1982 release under CFAO 19-20. I reasoned that by applying to a reserve CAF unit instead of the Regular Force again, I would avoid the intense medical examinations that would ultimately disqualify me from proceeding with enrolment because of HIV. Instead, by choosing the Cadet Instructor Cadre, a reserve component of the CAF, the medical would be completed by my own doctor.

After eight months of serving as a civilian volunteer pending re-enrolment, my CO called me and said she knew why my enrolment was taking so long. I was gay. Over the course of months of back and forth between the Regional HQ in Victoria and NDHQ in Ottawa, it was decided that the CAF would bring me into a recruiting centre and ask me if I was gay. Authorities let it be known to my CO, who conveyed this information to me, that when asked about my 1982 release, I was to tell the recruiting officer that I was young and it was all a mistake. At which point I could be re-enrolled. I told my CO to convey to

CFAO 19-20

OAFC 19-

HOMOSEXUALITY – SEXUAL ABNORMALITY INVESTIGATION, MEDICAL EXAMINATION AND DISPOSAL

Definition

1. For the purposes of this order:
   a. "homosexual" is one who has a sexual propensity for persons of one's own sex; and
   b. "sexual abnormality" is any form of sexual behaviour not conforming with accepted moral standards or constituting an offence under the Criminal Code of Canada, eg. voyeurism, exhibitionism, gross indecency, bestiality.

Investigation

2. If a person subject to the Code of Service Discipline becomes aware, or suspects that a member of the Canadian Forces (CF) is a homosexual, or has a sexual abnormality, he shall report the matter to the commanding officer (CO).

3. The CO shall investigate the report in whatever manner he deems appropriate. In making the investigation, he should make use of a medical officer (MO) and if necessary, the military police or any other means at his disposal. However, any investigation made pursuant to this order must be carefully managed so that innocent persons are not made to suffer, especially since the member under investigation may sometimes be the object of malice. The investigation and all subsequent action shall be conducted so that the subject will be caused minimal embarrassment. If a woman is involved, questioning other than by an MO shall be conducted in the presence of either a woman officer, preferably a nursing sister, or a military police woman; or, if neither is available, questioning shall be conducted in the presence of a woman non-commissioned officer.

4. If the investigation tends to substantiate the report, the CO shall:
   a. call in the local Special Investigation Unit (SIU) to investigate further; and
   b. when the MO so recommends, refer the subject for psychiatric examination.

HOMOSEXUALITÉ – ENQUÊTES SUR LA DÉVIATION SEXUELLE (EXAMEN MÉDICAL ET MESURES À PRENDRE)

Définition

1. Aux fins de la présente ordonnance:
   a. "homosexuel" désigne une personne qui éprouve une appétence sexuelle pour les individus de son propre sexe; et
   b. "déviation sexuelle" désigne toute forme de comportement sexuel qui s'oppose aux bonnes mœurs ou constitue une infraction en vertu du Code criminel du Canada, par exemple, le voyeurisme, l'exhibitionnisme, grossière indécence, la bestialité, etc.

Enquête

2. Toute personne assujettie au Code de discipline militaire qui découvre ou soupçonne qu'un militaire des Forces canadiennes (FC) est un homosexuel ou souffre d'une déviation sexuelle, doit en faire rapport au commandant.

3. Le commandant doit faire enquête sur ce rapport de la manière qu'il juge opportune. Au cours de l'enquête, il devrait avoir recours aux services d'un médecin militaire et si nécessaire, aux services de la police militaire ou tout autre moyen dont il dispose. Cependant, toute enquête menée en conformité de la présente ordonnance doit s'entourer des précautions voulues afin que les innocents n'aient pas à en subir les conséquences, surtout du fait que le militaire soupçonné peut quelquefois être l'objet d'intentions malveillantes. L'enquête et toute mesure subséquente devront être effectuées de façon à causer le moins de gêne possible à la personne concernée. Si une femme est impliquée, l'interrogatoire, sauf celui du médecin militaire, devra se faire en présence d'une femme officier, de préférence une infirmière ou un policier militaire membre du personnel féminin; si l'une ou l'autre de ces deux personnes n'est pas disponible, l'interrogatoire aura lieu en présence d'un sous-officier du personnel féminin.

4. Si l'enquête tend à confirmer le rapport, le commandant doit:
   a. faire venir l'Unité des enquêtes spéciales (UES) de la région pour effectuer une enquête plus approfondie; et
   b. lorsque le médecin militaire le recommande, faire subir un examen psychiatrique à la personne concernée.

authorities not to ask me anything about my sexuality, and I would not offer any information about being gay.

However, if asked, I would not lie. It was not lost on me that in 1982, when interrogated about my sexuality, I admitted my sexuality and for that I was released. Now in 1992, I was urged to go to the recruiting centre and lie that I wasn't gay, tell them it was all a mistake, and they would let me back in. A date was set for the interview, and I expected to be rejected at which point I was going to sue. I called Svend Robinson, at the time MP in Burnaby, and he counselled me and told me that there were other actions coming and that I should not lie at my interview.

In the weeks before my interview at the Vancouver recruiting centre in early November 1992, the Federal court ruled in the

Douglas v. Canada case and immediately, the CAF was ordered to cease discriminating against gays and I was re-enrolled. The Chief of Defence Staff at the time, General John De Chastelain, knew that the court order was coming, and acted as CDS and ordered the CAF to comply with the Federal Court ruling, and repealed CFAO 19-20 in a message issued from NDHQ October 27, 1992.

Unbeknownst to me at the time, the courageous Michelle Douglas, who had been purged from the CAF in 1989 as a Security Officer working for the SIU, had met Svend Robinson and Clayton Ruby and together, they challenged the Federal Government in court in 1991-1992. Svend Robinson, who

UNCLASSIFIED

01   271550 Z OCT 92 PP   UUUU   CDS 182

NDHQ OTTAWA//CDS//

CANFORGEN 54/92

CANRESGEN 28/92

UNCLAS CDS 182

SIC WAC

BILINGUAL MESSAGE/MESSAGE BILINGUE

SUBJ: HOMOSEXUAL CONDUCT

REF: CFAO 19-20

1. ON 27 OCT 92 THE FEDERAL COURT OF CANADA TRIAL DIVISION
DECLARED THAT POLICIES RESTRICTING THE SERVICE OF HOMOSEXUALS IN
THE CF ARE CONTRARY TO THE CANADIAN CHARTER OF RIGHTS AND FREEDOMS.
THEREFORE, CFAO 19-20 AND ALL INTERIM POLICIES UNDER THAT ORDER ARE
REVOKED IMMEDIATELY

2. WHILE THIS DECISION MAY BE DIFFICULT FOR SOME MEMBERS OF THE CF
TO ACCEPT, I WISH YOU ALL TO UNDERSTAND THAT REVOCATION OF THE
HOMOSEXUAL POLICY HAS MY FULL SUPPORT

3. THE CF HOMOSEXUAL POLICY WAS ONE WHICH REFLECTED LONG-STANDING
NATIONAL ATTITUDES TOWARDS HOMOSEXUALITY AND WAS CONSISTENT WITH
CANADIAN LEGISLATION PRIOR TO THE ENACTMENT OF THE CANADIAN CHARTER

UNCLASSIFIED

Reproduced from the LGTB Purge Fund web site. (Author's Collection)
eventually outed himself as the first gay MP in Canada, had
worked on the constitution committee in 1981 trying to
get sexual orientation included in the Charter of Rights and
Freedoms. Clayton Ruby was a constitutional lawyer in Toronto.
Svend Robinson managed to convince the Mulroney government
as early as 1985 to allow the Equality Rights Committee of the

Photo credit from my personal photo collection Me and Michelle Douglas at a Purge Presentation in Victoria BC in 2022.

Parliament of Canada to hear cases of discrimination against gays in the military, which they did. John Crosbie, a Conservative minister in government, announced in 1986 that the government would stop all discrimination based on sexual orientation. Despite these declarations, the Purge continued in the Canadian Forces, RCMP, and Federal Civil Service.

It's interesting to note that then Prime Minister Brian Mulroney stated in 1992 that the LGBT purges were "one of the great outrages and violations of fundamental human liberty that one would have seen for an extended period of time." Soon after, a settlement was reached in the Michelle Douglas case.

In the first weeks of November 1992, the call came from the Vancouver Recruiting Centre. For weeks I was uneasy at the upcoming interview and in my mind it was a showdown. To my astonishment, I was informed that my interview was now cancelled, and that I would be re-enrolled in the Cadet Instructor Cadre as a lieutenant effective immediately.

Documents later revealed to me as a result of the class action suit settlement of 2017, showed messages from Ottawa to Victoria HQ stating I was the first known homosexual re-enrolled after the policy reversal of October 1992.

Chapter 8

MY RETURN TO SERVICE

As things go, I have not died from HIV.

I offered myself as a human guinea pig for early anti-retroviral medications in the mid 1990s, and returned to work in 1998. I called the Great West Life Company and asked to be taken off long term disability payments. They were shocked. I went on for a further twelve years of service and rose to the rank of Lieutenant-Colonel in the Reserves. I "retired" early in 2013.

Resilience is one of the hallmark characteristics that are attributed to members of the Royal Canadian Air Force.

It has played a big part in life.

One of my proudest accomplishments in my return to uniform life is the creation of the Computerized Aircraft Simulation Centre or CASC.

When I returned to wearing the uniform as Lieutenant in the Cadet Instructor Cadre (CIC) of the Reserve Force, I was appointed training officer of 103 Thunderbird Squadron, Royal Canadian Air Cadets in North Vancouver.

The 103 is a storied Air Cadet squadron with lots of history and a proud record of service to the community.

I found an older flight simulator that had been donated to the squadron, and with my computer expertise honed at

Lt. Steven Deschamps in one of two Thrustmaster F-16 simulator cockpits I "procured" for 103 Thunderbird Squadron North Vancouver

IBM System school, my employer after being purged, I put it back together and started a program I called the Computerized Aircraft Simulation Centre. Using Microsoft Flight Simulator software and hardware such as throttles, yokes, and rudder pedals acquired from computer stores, I built a program to teach young Air Cadets as early as twelve years old, how to fly Cessna aircraft on simulators. The program caught on!

Over the years as a serving CIC officer, I volunteered thousands of hours teaching cadets how to fly, and my CASC program became the cornerstone of simulator complexes at Air Cadet squadrons throughout Canada.

Thousands of Air Cadets learned the rudimentary knowledge of how to fly on simulators using a set of fifteen lesson plans I created and published from the Ministry of Transportation pilot program.

Today, so many pilots around the world started their flying career in Air Cadets using CASC, including many of my students, some who are now captains of A380 or former Snowbirds. On Vancouver Island in 2024, there are over fifteen CASC simulators using Virtual Reality headsets to teach Air Cadets at six different squadrons.

Chapter 9

PTSD AND MENTAL HEALTH

I had done all I could do as a CIC lieutenant-colonel by 2013 and the total lack of career opportunities made me realize that I could no longer serve and retired at the age of fifty-eight. Compulsory release age is sixty-five for Reserve members. I believe I would have served to maximum pensionable age, retired with a very healthy pension, and most likely not have suffered from PTSD and depression most of my life if the events of 1982 had not happened.

Instead, I had to buy back my pensionable time when the government provided The Reserve Pension plan in 2008 or so.

I realized I could not work any longer in 2013. My retirement income was modest, I was an introvert, if not a hermit with depression still nagging at my door. I don't know how it is I have not succumbed to alcohol, drugs, suicide, or poverty as I know so many have that were purged. Somehow, I attribute it to luck. If anything, the events since the PM apology and through the writing of these documents, have only served to rub salt in the wound. The last three years were some of the darkest of my life and have made me feel more isolated, depressed, and withdrawn at times. I watched the OTV "Fruit Machine" documentary.

It prompted a terrible reaction in me. I've come to realize that I became anti-social and introverted soon after being purged.

Prior to 1982, I had an active social life with friends, college buddies, neighbours etc. After the purge, I trusted no one. I did not get close to work colleagues and immersed myself in pathological lying in order to hide from employers or straight people that I was gay. I changed employment frequently in order to cover the fact that I had no girlfriends. I felt I could only avoid so many parties or social invitations from coworkers or bosses before they would ask questions. I used my resourcefulness to find other employment often.

In 2005, I was at a three day customer gala at a very expensive hotel. I hid in my room most of the time. I had a high profile in the company I was working for, so would easily be known in the hallways.

Depression has been a consistent disabler for me since the purge. I gained weight in the 80s and ate poorly, often using food and alcohol to numb my pain. I slept ten to twelve hours a day and continue to require long sleep nights and naps.

I was suicidal after the purge. In fact, it seemed like the only productive thing I could do. I suffered silently, trapped in a non-life existence often thinking how things could have been different. I have suicidal thoughts very often, thinking of ways I could kill myself like pills, alcohol, bridges, or even, car accidents.

I have boxes of pictures, certificates, and plaques that I got as a cadet and Air Force officer leading up to my release. I boxed them up and never looked at them again because I believed they would bring back such a painful period and would trigger bouts of depression.

My attendance at work was sporadic. I would call in sick often and sometimes declare a mental health week, call in with some excuse to my employer, and stay home and hide.

Prior to 1982 and being released during the purge, I had a tall, slight build. My ID card photographs at my release show that I was 185 cm and 74 kg. Within two years of my release, I had slept, eaten, and drank myself to a weight close to 100 kg.

Bouts of this occur when painful memories resurface about my military career and its end during the Purge in 1982. I still wake up reliving events from the Purge. The office bullying, the interrogations, the lies, and obfuscation I was making to people about my past. I became very irritable after the Purge. I was always a very carefree kind of guy. I found myself being irritated by people for nothing at all.

In fact, the only credit I give myself is that somehow I've managed to survive this long, robbed of joy and purpose in life. I remember being proud of my service, my rank, my abilities, and my contributions to the Canadian Armed Forces and my society. I had an easy smile and was the life of the party. I remember being happy and waking up refreshed and eager for the day to begin.

I've had openly gay members serve under my command in my later career in the Reserves. I was always jealous that they could be so free and easy about being who they were. I've never been able to feel that way since the summer of 1982. For years after my release, I would have sleepless nights. I would lie in bed alone at night, sometimes in cold sweats, reliving the interrogation process. I would imagine myself in the chair, pouring over each question being asked, thinking how will this trap me? How will I betray my sexuality? How could my answers be benign? I remember thinking over and over why did this happen to me? I had served extraordinarily well. I was rated very well in performance, I had been given accelerated promotions in cadets, courses, and awards. I was a model military officer. Why were these two sergeants interrogating me? I still require sleeping pills to go to sleep more often than not. I often lie in bed, anxious, and will relive moments in time during my release. I will have flashbacks to being taunted at work by superiors I respected. I feel guilty for making fag jokes along with military buddies in order to hide my homosexuality and try to be like them.

I often wondered how I came on to the SIU radar for the Purge. It still haunts me. Now I believe I can thank the Intelligence community for that.

As far as mental health issues are concerned, there is no "one size fits all." It's important that those of us who finally realize we have suffered from PTSD, talk about our issues and the way we have suffered so others will understand as well. A friend of mine who volunteers on one of the boards we both serve on, was quoted as saying: "We are here to say, we exist, it was serious, it was a mistake, and giving us the help we need to fix ourselves is extremely important." She is right.

As I have been reliving the events that occurred around my release in June of 1982, I have had to take time to evaluate so many things. I have reached out to family and old friends to talk to them, sometimes asking them about what I was like back then, asking if they recall this or that and examining my life since the Purge.

Recently, I was in contact with an old cadet student and former colleague of mine, Rob. Our paths went different ways and we lost track of each other. When we reconnected on the phone in spring of 2024, Rob and I talked for hours. When he was young, he would call me from time to time to get advice and check in, as often we all do with mentors of ours. Rob reminded me of a conversation I had forgotten about. He called me in June of 1982, and apparently I was abrupt and dismissive. Rob pointed out that he realized after reading about my story, that he had called me right in the middle of the interrogations and SIU investigations. He told me that I was a changed man, and that he found my impatience totally uncharacteristic of me. We both realized just how much things changed for me in 1982.

It was a very difficult period of days doing the submission to the administrators for the class action suit. It has also been enlightening. In the end, My settlement case was adjudicated as Level 4, the highest of harm degrees afforded by the Purge.

Now I realize I'm a high functioning individual racked with problems. For the first time, I have pieced together so many of the events and things that happened, some of which I have repressed and forgotten about until now. I looked up PTSD on the web and realized that I have had most of the symptoms if not all since 1982. This book has made me think. What I have come to appreciate is how I think my life would have been completely different had I not been purged. That has created dire consequences over the years. I do not avoid responsibility; my drinking, my sexual misadventures, my suicidal thoughts, my shunning of people, my lack of love for myself are all things I have done. On the positive side, I have had an epiphany that I'm not a bad person, but bad things happened to me. Perhaps now I can start work on making life better.

I have contacted Veterans Affairs and they opened a case on me. With VA help, I was made a patient of the Operational Stress Injuries clinic here in Victoria. With VA help, I saw a psychologist for two hours every Monday in 2019 for five months.

As a result of therapy and talking about my experiences with other survivors, life has become much simpler lately. I have regained my confidence, and for the first time in years, I'm no longer taking anti-depression medication.

The Operational Stress Clinicians from Veterans Affairs started me on Prolonged Exposure Therapy in May 2024. For PTSD patients, we survive by not allowing ourselves to feel our pain. We learn to repress, bottle it up, to stop feeling the pain. I've learned that when you do that, you often stop feeling joy and love. Prolonged Exposure therapy is designed to help someone with PTSD to re-learn how to feel again. If this resonates with you, ask your clinician about it.

As I watch the unfolding of the Black Lives Matter and Residential School saga of other dark history, I wonder how much more is hidden to us Canadians by our governments. The Prime Minister's apology to Purge Survivors in 2017 was cathartic and for me and the start of healing. I totally empathize with other survivors who are calling for apologies from the highest authorities.

What is left to be explained in this story is how did the Purge actually start? How did a clandestine organization whose purpose within the RCMP and CAF was to persecute gays and lesbians, become a reality? How was it kept so secret and so immune from political interference and how did it act in such an un-Canadian fashion?

A copy of all the secret records held by the government on Steven Deschamps, released to me under the settlement terms of the 2017 Class Action Suit, have been donated to the War Museum of Canada archives. The documents point to a number of interesting facts that were never revealed to me during the interrogations. The SIU in Winnipeg, after analyzing the anonymous letter, concluded that the letter was not written by a teenager or a cadet. They concluded that the military form of the letter was beyond the ability of a young cadet. In addition, they interviewed dozens of people in Winnipeg and concluded that I was never around any cadets, as alleged in the anonymous letter. Their notes did not offer any conclusions as to the origin of the anonymous letter.

The last sentence in the letter is interesting: "I've made one additional copy of this letter to be sent to the Prime Minister's office IN PRIVACY if no action is taken." Why would that be written in the letter? Surely informing elected officials would be the right thing to do? Why would the author of the anonymous letter make a curious statement unless it was to leave a clue, that would never be unraveled until forty years later. I threatened to report the US operative "Major Jim Crawley" to the Prime Minister back in college days when I was being recruited to hunt down communist sympathizers. I wonder if the intelligence/security community in Canada was playing cat and mouse with me as retaliation and leaving sinister clues behind.

Another curious fact revealed to me from the SIU secret files was the SIU Winnipeg had concluded there was no basis to the allegations that I was gay and forwarded the files to SIU Ottawa to close them. SIU Ottawa decided to interview me anyway and the results were cataclysmic. If I could have consulted legal counsel, no interrogations or further military action would have come my way. However, denied the right to counsel, well the rest is history.

I only wish I could have had the life I was loving back in 1982 before this all happened.

Chapter 10

CANADA PRIDE CITATION

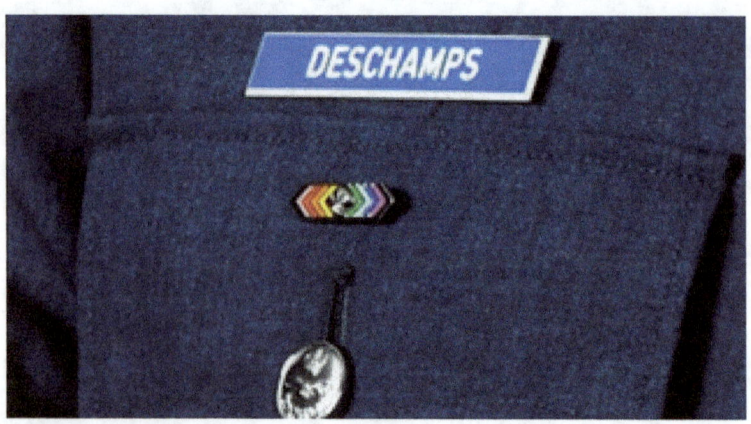

On the day Prime Minister Justin Trudeau rose in the House of Commons in the fall of 2017, I watched the apology live, alone in my living room in Victoria. I choked, and at one point, sobbed uncontrollably. It's the first time I can remember crying like that since the death of my mother. I had joined the class action suit against the Government of Canada regarding the Purge. The settlement provided for roughly $145 million dollars, 20 to 30 million of it to be put aside for memorialization and education.

The pride citation was to be the physical form of recognition and was to be presented to each member of the class action

CANADA PRIDE CITATION
CITATION FIERTÉ CANADA

Public Register of Arms, Flags and Badges of Canada
Registre public des armoiries, drapeaux et insignes du Canada
Volume VII, page 129, 20 December / décembre 2018

Chief Herald of Canada   Héraut d'armes du Canada

suit. It came in two forms: a lapel pin and a military bar that would be worn on the uniform if you were still serving.

Change of appointment ceremony at 442 (MH) Squadron on 19 April, 2023. (CFB Esquimalt Imaging Unit)

The pride citation was conceived and we were informed about it in 2018. I remember thinking that there could not be very many, if any, currently serving in the military who would receive the citation and actually wear it on their uniform. So in 2018, at the age of sixty-three, I sent an email to the Chief of Defence Staff (CDS), General Vance, offering my service to re-enrol for the two years I could serve before the compulsory release age of sixty-five. I reasoned that by being back in uniform, I could be used wherever an educational opportunity arose, to speak to my experience as a serving member. I thought I might be the only member still alive with the Pride Citation on my uniform.

I received my Pride Citation by courier in June 2020. The letter accompanying it from the CDS was very apologetic. As a result of the COVID-19 pandemic, the opportunity to present the citation in person was limited, but a date would be set, as soon as it was safe to do so, to formally present the citation to me and the others. In the meantime, the CAF leadership reasoned it was better to have the pins sitting in the recipients hands than stuffed in envelopes waiting for a future presentation date.

VAdm Angus Topshee, Commander of the RCN, presents me the Canada Pride Citation 18 April 2023. (CFB Esquimalt Imaging Unit)

I got a call from the Commander of the RCAF in July 2020, and we spoke for almost an hour. He was very interested in my story and offered to buy me lunch in Victoria when he was going to be there in August.

True to his word, The Commander of the RCAF and the Command Chief Warrant Officer, his executive assistant and I had lunch near the airport. During that time, LGen Meinzinger suggested I would be a good candidate for an Honorary Colonel position, a ceremonial position in Canada, where people are made a colonel in uniform of the RCAF, accorded all the honours and privileges of the position, but not made part of the chain of command, nor paid. I was delighted! The opportunity was presented to tell my story, as perhaps, the only serving uniformed member in the CAF wearing the Pride Citation.

I was appointed Honorary Colonel by the Minister of National Defence in November 2022, and was accepted as HCol of 443 (Maritime Helicopter) Squadron in April 2023.

Chapter 11

THE PURGE

The Purge exists as a dark chapter of our Canadian history. Starting as early as the 1950s, our government saw gay people as having "character defects" and as security risks.

The Cold War era saw Soviet defectors like Igor Gouzenko reveal the Soviets had extensive spy networks in Canada. Before 1969, homosexuality was illegal. The government systematically purged thousands of Canadians from the Federal Civil Service, the RCMP and the Canadian Armed Forces.

The RCMP had as many as 30,000 Canadians under surveillance during these times. The RCMP had classifications: suspected, alleged, or confirmed. If you were confirmed, action would be taken to remove you from any position within government, RCMP, or CAF. As many as 9000 people were purged from the CAF alone.

John Watkins was our Ambassador to the Soviet Union from 1954 to 1956. The Soviets set him up with a Soviet male homosexual and attempted to blackmail Watkins, but failed. The RCMP interrogated him in Montreal in 1964, and while under interrogation by the RCMP, he had a heart attack and died. The RCMP and Government refused to release the files of this murder.

In an attempt to bring science to the shady investigation in the 1960s, the government funded a scientific project designed to have the ability to detect homosexuality using perspiration, heart rates, and eye movement when presented with male nude photographs. The experiment failed miserably and was dubbed the "Fruit Machine" by a lead RCMP sergeant in charge of investigating homosexuals.

The Purge officially ended in 1992 when Michelle Douglas sued the Canadian Armed Forces with Clayton Ruby as her lawyer. The settlement saw the repeal of CFAO 19-20 in CAF, ending discriminatory practices in the government of Canada.

A disproportionate number of females were purged from the CAF in the 70s and 80s leading me to believe that the system was off the rails and purging anyone the male caucasian establishment in the CAF at the time deemed a "threat." A disproportionate number of Purge survivors that joined the Class Action Suit in 2017 were female.

In 2017, Prime Minister Justin Trudeau gave an official apology in the House of Commons for the Gay Purge.

At that same time, the Government announced a settlement of $145 million for a class action suit led by Douglas Elliot, a lawyer and longtime gay rights activist. $110 million would be used for individual compensation to the approximately 715 Purge survivor litigants, the rest to be administered by the Purge Fund for reconciliation and memorialization. Some of these projects include YouTube testimonials from Purge survivors (search for LGTB Purge - Survivors Stories), a National Monument for commemorating Purge survivors, in Ottawa, and a major display at the Canadian Museum for Human Rights in Winnipeg.

CHAPTER 12

EPILOGUE

Since the apology in 2017, I have found myself increasingly confident about telling my story. Since 2020, I've joined a number of high profile organizations in hopes of being able to contribute from first hand experience. I am the founding President of the Cadet Instructor Branch Association of British Columbia, Director of Rainbow Veterans of Canada, a member of the Advisory Council of the Canadian Human Rights Museum, a member of the Advisory Group to the Minister of Veterans Affairs, and Honorary Colonel of 443 (MH) Squadron.

A display dedicated to the Purge features myself and Diane Pitre, founder of Rainbow Veterans of Canada, at the National Aviation and Space Museum in Ottawa.

I am also featured in *Pathway to the Stars*, the 100th anniversary book of the RCAF.

Diane Pitre and myself at Vancouver Military Dinner fundraiser for Rainbow Veterans of Canada. (Author's Collection)

In 2024, The Governor General's office informed me I am the recipient of the Sovereign's Medal for Volunteers for volunteer work with the CIC Association of BC which I founded and the thousands of hours building the Computerized Aircraft Simulation System (CASC) and teaching air cadets how to fly on simulators.

Warpath Press is dedicated to publishing the very best in military writing from around the globe.

We believe that writing that is rooted in the human experience of war and conflict, even when written by non-veterans, allows us as a society to examine how human nature responds under extreme pressure. It also gives us a means to ask the big questions about life.

"Military stories" aren't all action-adventure novels. We are committed to finding ways to push the boundaries of "military writing" in new directions, bending it into new shapes that serve society in better ways.

Many of the literary greats of the early to mid-20th century wrote about war and its effects. But Hemingway, Remarque, Dos Passos, Faulkner, Wouk, Greene and Waugh, only had the impact that they did because they were published.

Today, they would likely have been ignored by the major publishers.

And that is why we do what we do.

To learn more about the Purge, go to
https://rainbowveterans.ca/
or
http://www.deschamps.org/

www.ingramcontent.com/pod-product-compliance
Lightning Source LLC
Chambersburg PA
CBHW071216120626
46546CB00006B/2587